FINDING A JOB WHEN JOBS ARE HARD TO FIND

OTHER BOOKS BY THE AUTHORS

Jurg Oppliger

Job Power: Choose your Career
Job Power: Master the Job Search
Job Power: Ace the Interview
Get that Job
Sell More

John Drake

Downshifting—How to Work Less and Enjoy Life More
The Perfect Interview
The Effective Interviewer
Interviewing for Managers
Performance Appraisal—One More Time
The New Cook's Cookbook (S. Milardo, co-author)
Golf for the 60+ Crowd

JURG OPPLIGER & JOHN DRAKE

THE SECRETS OF SUCCESS
FINDING A JOB WHEN JOBS ARE HARD TO FIND

TATE PUBLISHING
AND ENTERPRISES, LLC

Finding a Job When Jobs Are Hard to Find
Copyright © 2015 by Jurg Oppliger and John Drake. All rights reserved.

No part of this publication may be reproduced, stored in a retrieval system or transmitted in any way by any means, electronic, mechanical, photocopy, recording or otherwise without the prior permission of the author except as provided by USA copyright law.

The opinions expressed by the author are not necessarily those of Tate Publishing, LLC.

This publication is written to provide accurate and authoritative information in regard to job search. However, it is distributed on an "as is" basis with the understanding that each individual and each job situation is unique and that each reader takes full responsibility for the outcome of recommendations provided herein, and that the authors and publisher shall not have any liability to any person or entity with respect to loss or damage caused directly or indirectly by the recommendations provided in this book. The authors are not engaged in rendering legal or professional counseling services. If such services are needed, appropriate professionals should be sought.

Published by Tate Publishing & Enterprises, LLC
127 E. Trade Center Terrace | Mustang, Oklahoma 73064 USA
1.888.361.9473 | www.tatepublishing.com

Tate Publishing is committed to excellence in the publishing industry. The company reflects the philosophy established by the founders, based on Psalm 68:11,
"The Lord gave the word and great was the company of those who published it."

Book design copyright © 2015 by Tate Publishing, LLC. All rights reserved.
Cover design by Joseph Emnace
Interior design by Jake Muelle

Published in the United States of America

ISBN: 978-1-62563-658-4
1. Self-Help / Personal Growth / Success
2. Business & Economics / Careers / Job Hunting
14.11.20

Dedicated to

all the men and women who wish to work,
but cannot find a job.

Contents

Introduction 13

Chapter 1 Control Cost 17

Chapter 2 How to Use This Book 21

Chapter 3 What I Have to Offer 23

Chapter 4 My Ideal Job 35

Chapter 5 What is the Current Job Market? 39

Chapter 6 My Resume 43

Chapter 7 My Cover Letter 61

Chapter 8 The Five Ways to Get a Job............ 65

Chapter 9 Getting the Job—
 Networking Face to Face............... 71

Chapter 10 Getting the Job—
 Networking with the Internet 85

Chapter 11 Getting the Job—Personal Solicitation ... 89

Chapter 12 Getting the Job—Target Letters 93

Chapter 13 Getting the Job—Newspaper Ads....... 99

Chapter 14 Getting the Job—
          Internet Applications................ 103

Chapter 15 My Work Plan..................... 107

Chapter 16 My Job Interview 115

Chapter 17 My start in the New Company 149

Skillbuilders

1. Listing of Job Search Expenses. 19
2. What I Like to Do 25
3. My Success Stories 27
4. My Special Knowledge 30
5. My Five Best Strengths 32
6. My Ideal Job. 38
7. Networking Contacts 79
8. Networking Contacts—Notebook Lists 81
9. My Workplan 109
10. Networking Contact Card 111
11. Company Contact Card 113
12. Cataloging Your Strengths Developing "One-Liners" 137
13. Shaping Answers to the Invitation: "Tell Me About Yourself". 140
14. Answering the "Weaknesses" Question. 143
15. Lessons From Your Interview. 145

Sample Documents

Resume A	53
Resume B	55
Resume C	57
Cover Letter	63
Target Letter	96
Application to a Newspaper Ad	101

Introduction

In today's very difficult job market, the secret that makes the difference between success and failure comes down to three things, no matter if you are a New Graduate, an Experienced Job Seeker, a Baby Boomer, or a Senior. They are:

- *Positive Attitude*
- *Successful Approach*
- *Proven Tools.*

This "how-to" book differs from other job search books in that it focuses on these three elements.

The Positive Attitude is gained by working through Chapter Three: "What I Have to Offer." Here you will learn how to determine your real interests, where you had successes in the past, and your positive strengths and qualities. This will provide the self confidence necessary to have a successful attitude, which in turn, will help you to write a convincing resume and to score well in interviews.

The Successful Approach is based on understanding the current Job Market: You learn about this in Chapter Five. This leads you to a mixture of five ways to approach potential employers, which is explained in chapters nine to fourteen. Selecting the right approaches is crucial to shortening the time needed to succeed.

The Proven Tools are the keys to success. Your first tool is Your Resume. Your resume has to sell you, but leave enough questions open so that the employer wants to see you. In Chapter Six we teach you how to write an irresistible resume that will get you scheduled for an interview.

The second tool is Your Interview. You will learn in Chapter Sixteen how to prepare yourself very carefully for your first interview, and then to analyze it, eliminate the mistakes, and add whatever you found missing. Following our procedures, every interview will be better than the previous one.

For readers over 50, each chapter includes a section devoted to your special situation. It shows 50+ applicants not only how to minimize the negative aspects of their age, but also how to capitalize of the advantages of their longer work experience.

As we have indicated before, job hunting in today's market is not easy. You will quickly learn that...

Looking for a job is a full time job!

But don't be too concerned; we are here to walk you each step of the way–from defining yourself and defining the right job to managing the first days in your new position.

We're about to begin a journey together. Welcome aboard!

1

Control Cost

Before we begin our journey to a new job, we'll look at an important step that can save you money.

This chapter has to do with the dollars you spend during your job search process. When you consider telephone, printing, and travel expenses, it can add up to a fairly substantial sum. The good news is that your job search expenses are tax deductible. Every dollar spent can be used to reduce your income taxes.

So, beginning right now, start to keep a record of all job search expenses. Your first item can be the cost of this book!

We recommend use of a small notebook that is easy to carry with you. As you incur an expense, jot it down ASAP. *Be sure to save each receipt.* Another approach is to use the Worksheet provided with this chapter. In either case, maintain a folder for your receipts so that you can support your IRS deductions (should you ever be challenged).

Here are some expenses that you should record:

- Paper and envelopes
- Printer toner and inks
- Postage
- Telephone calls
- Faxes
- Many publications (newspapers, magazines, etc) used for your job search
- Memberships used to widen job search
- Meals while networking and traveling to interviews
- Transportation costs—planes, trains, taxi, etc.
- Purchase of computer or printer purchased during your job search (check tax rules to determine how much can be deducted).

On the next page is a handy format for recording your expenses.

Go to www.jobsearchskillbuilders.com, download and print this form or all other Skillbuilders.

Skillbuilder 1

Listing of Job Search Expenses

Date *Purpose* *Amount*

2

How to Use This Book

This book was designed to be an easy-to-use handbook. It describes a proven, systematic process for getting a job. You will benefit most from the contents by following a few simple steps:

- *Read the whole book first.* Having a sense of the "big picture" will help you understand how one chapter builds upon the next. Then start to work through the book.

- *Follow each chapter in the order presented.* The Worksheets (called Skillbuilders) provided with the chapters help you build strengths that will be used in subsequent chapters. It's like building a ladder to the job—you start at the base and add rungs that lead you up to the employment interview.

- *Complete all the Skillbuilders.* These are useful documents. You will refer to them frequently as you conduct your job campaign. They also will help you design your resume, network effectively, and experience success in your job interviews.

Right now, turn to the Table of Contents; it will provide a quick overview of the road we'll be traveling together.

You Will Succeed If You Start Now!

3

What I Have to Offer

In seeking a job, what do you bring to the table? It's important to know the answer to this question so that you end up with a job in which you will be successful and that gives you satisfaction.

This chapter is designed to help you think about the kind of attributes you can provide a prospective employer—the kind of information you can draw upon when preparing your resume and taking interviews. You will find that doing the exercises in this chapter is an upbeat activity, especially if you are feeling discouraged about job prospects. It asks you to bring forward the best of you and your talents.

We are going to suggest that you analyze yourself from three perspectives:

- *Your Interests*—what you like doing and find satisfying

- *Your Special Skills*—your talents and abilities
- *Your Knowledge Base*—your special know-how.

My Interests

Let's begin with your interests—what you like to do. Let's see if you can pinpoint what needs to be in a job for you to enjoy it.

One way to get a "feel" for what satisfies is to daydream a little. Think about your last job (part-time or full-time). When you were most happy at work, what was it you were doing? It might be interesting, too, to ask your spouse or close friends when they saw you happiest or pleased about your work.

Using this overview as a base, let's now try to define, more specifically, what may have accounted for your job satisfaction. Please go now to Skillbuilder 2 and complete the brief questionnaire. When you've finished the worksheet, move on to My Special Skills.

Skillbuilder 2

What I Like to Do

(Check as many as fit you)		
Activity	*Yes*	*No*
Work as part of a team	—	—
Work independently	—	—
Work as a supervisor or manager	—	—
Work with my hands—manual work	—	—
Work with ideas—creative thinking	—	—
Work with others in a helpful, counseling way	—	—
Work in an organized, systematic way	—	—
Work in a fast-paced, action-oriented setting	—	—
Work at persuading others, for example sales	—	—

Other preferences: _____

Now look over your checkmarks and comment. Any common threads?

All told, it seems that I like jobs that allow me to:

_____
_____
_____

My Special Skills

Now, let's look at your skills and abilities. You can start by thinking about your past successes—in school, in your private life and/or at work. These were occasions when you were proud of yourself or times when you were complimented by your supervisor, teacher, family, or friends. This information will be most helpful when you prepare your resume and take job interviews.

A productive way to stimulate your thinking about these important attributes is to write your "success stories." A good success story has three parts:

1. Describe a problem or task
2. What you did about it
3. The end result of your efforts

In Skillbuilder 3 you will find spaces to record your stories. This is an important exercise; you might be surprised about the insights you gain.

Skillbuilder 3

My Success Stories

Story #1
Problem _____
_____
_____

Action I took _____
_____
_____

Results _____
_____
_____

Story # 2
Problem _____
_____
_____

Action I took _____
_____
_____

Results _____
_____
_____

Story # 3
Problem _____

_____

_____

Action I took _____

_____

_____

Results _____

_____

_____

_____

_____

My Knowledge Base

In school and in your past jobs, you have acquired much "know-how." So, let's analyze that knowledge base and look for specifics that you know how to do well. For example, here are some things that people might say:

I have good knowledge when it comes to:

1. Computer work (Word, Excel, PowerPoint, etc.)
2. Internet use
3. Accounting/finance
4. Training/teaching others
5. Selling
6. Car repair
7. Real estate markets
8. Pediatric nursing
9. Management strategies
10. Electric wiring

Now how about you? On Skillbuilder 4 list all the specific topics for which you have solid, working knowledge. It's OK to list know-how in topics unrelated to your work. The main thing is to be as comprehensive as you can.

Skillbuilder 4

My Special Knowledge

1. _____

2. _____

3. _____

4. _____

5. _____

6. _____

7. _____

8. _____

An Overview—My Strengths and Qualities

Looking back over Skillbuilders 2, 3, and 4, what interests, talents, skill, aptitudes, or know-how stand out? These are your *strong* attributes—the qualities that are likely to be meaningful to an employer.

To focus on these key qualities, write down, in Skillbuilder 5, five of the strongest assets that you have uncovered. You can confirm this list, and maybe even add to it, by asking yourself what your co-workers, supervisors, friends, or your family would offer. We know someone who says, "The best way to answer this assets question is to think what orators would say at your funeral."

If you are over Fifty

You have some characteristics that younger job candidates may not have to the same extent:

- *Experience, maturity, steadiness, loyalty (if your track record backs that up), and high work ethics.*
- *Stability. Younger employees are apt to change jobs more often. Those over 50 are less likely to move about.*

You do not want to draw attention to your age, therefore be careful how you use these words on your resume and during any interview.

Skillbuilder 5

My Five Best Strengths

1. _____

2. _____

3. _____

4. _____

5. _____

The strengths you have recorded here will be most useful when are preparing for your interview (Chapter 16). You might even want to take a quick look at that chapter to see how they will be used.

Key Points

- Most likely you have many more strengths than you realize.
- Bringing these attributes to the surface and feeling comfortable with them is an important step in resume preparation and in conducting successful interviews.
- We believe it important to analyze your specific strengths in three categories: your interests, your skills and talents, and your knowledge base.
- You want to be able to talk easily and confidently about these strengths. In Chapter 16, we'll show you how.

4

My Ideal Job

In this chapter, we will help you define your "Ideal Job." We will accomplish this by determining your ideal company, ideal work, ideal pay, and ideal perks. To assist you with this, you will find Skillbuilder 6 at the end of this chapter.

Will you find this "Ideal Job"? Most probably not; you will have to make concessions—but concessions from what?

Once you have defined your ideal job, you will have a "yardstick" against which to compare jobs offered to you. In turn, this will help you decide which ones you want to go for. This is an important chapter for defining your career path.

Job Description

What kind of a company would you like to work for? A big national corporation, a local company, a very small company?

What industry do you know best? What industry are you most interested in?

What kind of tasks do you want to perform?

What level of responsibility do you want: manage a whole company—manage a department, supervise a group of people, or perform a non-supervisory job?

Job Conditions

What hours do you want to work: Early shift, late shift, night shift, weekends, or a typical 8-5 day?

Are you willing to relocate?

How far are you willing to travel every day to work?

How much overnight traveling do you want? (none, occasional, regularly)

Pay and benefits

What minimum salary do you need?

Are you looking for a weekly salary or are you willing to work for an hourly fee?

Would you work for straight commission only?

If a part of your income would be a commission or bonus, how much do you need for the fixed income part?

How about health benefits, a retirement plan, vacations?

Growth Potential

How important are promotion possibilities to you?

What is your Ten Year Plan in view of location, position, salary?

> *If you are over Fifty*
>
> *With your many years of work, you gained quite some experience that lets you make a good decision. You know from experience what you are good at, and what gives you most satisfaction.*
>
> *Decide how many years you still want to or have to work. Keep in mind that your physical abilities may decline. You have other assets, such as experience and maturity.*

Skillbuilder 6

My Ideal Job

Description _____
_____
_____
_____

Conditions _____
_____
_____
_____

Pay and Benefits _____
_____
_____
_____

Growth Potential _____
_____
_____
_____

5

What is the Current Job Market?

The Public Job Market

The "Public Job Market" consists of all jobs that are offered to everybody through the internet, newspapers, or magazines. An amazing quantity of jobs is offered this way. But, because we have a high unemployment rate and almost everybody can access these offers, there is also much competition. It is not unusual that several hundred applications are received for one job!

The Hidden Job Market

The "Hidden Job Market" consists of all the jobs that are not offered to the public, but are filled through personal contacts (friends or relatives), by present employees of the company (through transfers or promotions), or by coincidence. Nobody knows exactly how many jobs are available this way, but we estimate that about three quarters of the jobs are filled via this market.

This tells you that Networking, Personal Solicitation, and Target Letters are the best approaches to find a job!

In Chapter 8 we will show you how to access both the Public Job Market and the more interesting Hidden Job Market.

Working at Home

On the Internet you find a great number of offers to get rich quickly by working at home. Almost all of these are scams. Be very careful or you will lose your money.

Here are some working at home options that seem to be reliable.

>   MyOnLineIncomeSystem
>   Maverick Money Makers
>   Top Paying Surveys

Caution: While we believe those firms are OK, situations change and, therefore, your own investigation is necessary. It is your decision.

If you are over Fifty
  Some industries or kinds of business are more age friendly and likely to hire people over 50:

- *Retail Grocery*
- *Financial Services*
- *Transportation*
- *Nonprofit Organizations*
- *Temporary Staffing Companies*
- *Government: IRS, Census Bureau, Homeland Security, and Veterans Adm.*
- *Health Care*
- *Home Care*

In general, small companies are more open than big corporations to hire older persons. But there are exceptions. Here's a list of "Age Friendly" companies.

AT&T
Best Buy
Borders
Bank of America
Chase

Google
H & R Block
Hertz
Home Depot
IRS
Kelly Services
Macy's
Manpower
Peace Corps
Sprint
Staples
Starbucks
Toys "R" us
Travelers
Talbots
Target
UPS
Verizon
Wachovia
Wells Fargo

6

My Resume

What is a resume for?

Your resume is the most important document in your job search. You will use it throughout your job search. Your resume will not bring you a job—only an interview will do this. But a good resume will give you a chance to be interviewed.

Your resume is a snapshot of you, your skills, and your experience. The purpose of your resume is:

1. To be read! It will only be read if it is short, maximum one page, and if the first few lines are interesting.

2. To make the reader want to see you. Mention things that spur the reader to want to know more.

3. To get an interview.

Some sample resumes are given at the end of this chapter.

You can also find examples of resumes for different positions on the internet at "www.career-advice.monster.com". Go to "resumes and letters", then "resume samples". They are good examples, but some of them are, in our opinion, too long.

Key Words

More and more companies are using electronic resume scanners. These programs search for specific words—key words—in resumes. If they do not find them, your resume may be discarded.

It is therefore important when applying for a job with a major company, with a recruiting agency, a headhunter, or the government, to put keywords in your resume.

You can find lists of keywords in the following two websites:

> www.resume-help.org/resume_action_words.htm
> www.enetsc.com/ResumeTips26.htm

You should create a basic resume, but be prepared to change it depending on the potential employer. In every job offer you will find keywords that touch on topics of importance to your potential employer. You should also use the exact same keywords in your cover letter.

Try to select powerful verbs to describe what you did or how you function. Here are some verbs that you may consider:

- Accomplished
- Collaborated
- Constructed
- Created
- Designed
- Developed
- Drafted
- Expanded
- Formulated
- Implemented
- Improved
- Initiated
- Launched
- Managed
- Negotiated
- Presented
- Produced
- Streamlined

- Supervised
- Wrote

How to structure your resume

The parts of a resume are
Your name, address, phone numbers and email address

- The Summary
- Your Work Experience
- Your Education
- Additional information

The next step is to collect all the information you need and then write a draft of the resume. This is a very important document, so spend quite some time working on it. Consider showing it to relatives and friends before you finalize it. Even so, you may want to change it after some interviews. This is a "live" document. Even if it is good, it can always be made better.

Just keep in mind: You cannot have a resume that pleases everybody. Your resume may appeal to one person, but not at all to another. Most important is that it appeals to you and shows a real picture of you.

Letters of Reference

Letters of Reference from former employers are an extra perk and, if you have one, should accompany the resume.

If you are over Fifty
  Nobody asks you for your age, so do not volunteer it.
  Do not give the year of your graduations
  In your job history, list only the jobs of the last fifteen to twenty years.

  Do not provide your driver's license number. In some states the last two digits of your year of birth are a part of the driver's license number.

  Show that you have energy: Mention sports you play, volunteer work, and physical activities in your home or garden.

  If you are not familiar with computers, take some software courses. You should be skillful at least with Microsoft Word and Excel.

In review, the resume has four basic parts. They are:

- The Summary
- Your work experience
- Your education
- Additional information

The Summary

In a Human Resources department, the person having a first look at your resume will not spend more than thirty seconds to determine if your case deserves a follow up. This is why the summary is very important.

It tells in a maximum of six lines who you are and what you can do. It determines if your resume will be read or put on the "no interest" pile.

Mention the strong points of your personality, the job you want, and your professional proficiencies. Here are three examples:

"A reliable, entrepreneurial manager experienced in sales and finance, very systematic and organized. Proficient in modern office procedures and software. A reliable hard worker with excellent listening and communication skills who relates well with people in stressful situations. Fluent in Spanish and French."

"A people oriented, dynamic, hardworking, and courteous individual with excellent communications skills and the ability to be flexible and calm in a fast-paced environment. Experienced in customer service relations and all aspects of dealing with the public."

"Honest, reliable, and productive worker with supermarket supervisory experience. Nine years successful work in the grocery industry as cashier and head clerk. Excellent reputation and recommendations as competent, knowledgeable, and helpful."

My Work Experience

Here you tell *what you did*, listing your past jobs.

For each job, provide whenever possible, the following information:

- Dates of your employment
- Name and location of the company
- Job title or function
- Tasks or responsibilities
- Successes on the job

Some examples:

1995–1999   Airdale Supermarket, Jacksonville, Florida
Improved the daily "Cashier's Report", was named best worker in the shop in 1998

2000–2003   The Mayflower Hotel, Casco, Maine
payable and receivable, payroll for 150 employees, monthly reporting. Cut the time for monthly reports from 16 to 4 days.

My Education

Do not start with elementary education. Refer only to high school, college, postgraduate courses, or special training sessions by former employers.

Example:

> Kennebunk High School Graduate 2006
> Certified Nurses Certificate 2009

Additional information

This includes items such as time in the Army, Navy, Air Force, Coast Guard or National Guard, books or newspaper/magazine articles you wrote, licenses, honors or awards, membership in clubs or associations, volunteer work you do or did. Only mention things that may be relevant to the job you are applying for or reflect positively upon your personality and/or skills.

Sample Document 1

Resume A

Peter Smith
109 Maine Street, St. Augustine, FL 32080
Phone 904 940 1234
Email psmith222@ yahoo.com

Summary

A conscientious, reliable hard worker who relates well with others—excellent listening and communications skills. Very good public speaker and counselor.

Fluent in English and Spanish.

Experienced user of Word, Excel, PowerPoint, and QuickBooks.

Professional career

2003 to 2008   *The Wonderful Hotel*, Kennebunkport, Maine

Chief Financial Officer.

With two accountants ran all financial transactions, including payroll for 140 employees, and weekly, monthly, and

	annual reports for the General Manager and the Board of Directors
2001 to 2003	*Real Estate Broker*, Kennebunk, Maine
	Independent
1993 to 2001	*Summer Playhouse*, Casco, Maine, summer theatre
	Business Manager, CFO and Accounting Manager
	Responsible for the "Non-artistic" running of the theatre
1988 to 1993	*Rocky Plumbing Inc.*, Ogunquit, Maine
	Accountant, accounts payable and receivable, petty cash
Education	Graduated from Woodside High School, Woodside, NY 1984
	Various college level accounting and finance courses at Hofstra University.
Military Service	1984 to 1988, US Air Force, PFC

Sample Document 2

Resume B

Tyrone Thomas
123 Sea Road, Uptown, NY 12345
Phone (518) 555 7890
Email TThomas12@ yahoo.com

Summary

Honest, reliable, and productive worker seeking a position as supermarket manager trainee. Nine years experience in the grocery industry as cashier, checker, and head clerk. Excellent reputation with customers and management as competent, knowledgeable, and helpful. Proficient with Microsoft Word and Excel.

Professional career

2001 to now   *Rusann's Food Market*, Spokana, NY

Assistant Manager, involved in recruiting, supervision, inventory control, and accounting.

Leaving because there is no possibility for development.

1998–2001   *Coop Supermarket*, Woodstock, NY

                         Retail Clerk and Cashier, trained new employees to become cashiers.

1995–1998   *Capwells*, Hartford, NY

                         Grocery buyer's assistant, learned to know all major regional and national suppliers, built up a data bank for all major products.

Education

                         Woodside High School, Woodside, NY, class of 1992

                         Binghampton Junior College, Binghampton, NY

                         Currently taking night-classes in Business Administration.

Military Service   US Air Force, 1992-1995

Sample Document 3

Resume C

Robert L. Johnson
177 Fairmount Avenue
Anytown, ME 01234
Phone: (123) 456 7891
Email: Error! Hyperlink reference not valid.

Summary

HR executive with strong IT capabilities and extensive union negotiation experience. Also, broad experience in manpower planning and force reduction. A hostile takeover of the firm leads me to seek employment elsewhere.

Professional Career

2005–2010   *VP Human Resources*, World Electronics, Inc. Directed all HR operations—headquarters and 6 plants (over 13,000 employees). In addition to administrative duties, served as chief contract negotiator with three unions, including IBEW and Machinist. In 2008 negotiations resulted in 18% ($38,000,000) reduction in labor costs. Upgraded HR

IT systems, providing faster, more accurate data with 10% reduction in HR staff. Served on Corporate Long Range Planning Committee.

2002–2005 *Director, Manpower Planning*, World Electronics Designed and implemented plan to downsize personnel in all plants (1,200 employees) and engineered merger of two plants. Developed compensation package for all involved.

1997–2002 HR Manager, Boston National Bank (Assets 2 B, 163 offices). Supervised HQ's Department of 10. Responsible for: staffing, compensation and benefits, training & development, performance management. Designed and implemented bank-wide performance management system. Implemented new IT system, consolidating all human resource records.

1995–1997 Technical Recruiter, Ingersoll-Rand. Developed "Recruiting Package". Trained management recruiters on interviewing and recruiting strategies. Over 2-year period, recruited over 170 engineers and other hi-tech personnel.

Education	MBA, Dartmouth Tuck School 1995
	BA, Rutgers University, 1993. 3.6 GPA, varsity sports
Personal	Married, 3 children

How to format and present your resume

- Print on superior quality white or cream paper 25 or 30 lb. The first impression your resume makes, even before it is read, comes from the fingers! A superior paper makes a superior impression.
- Use a good laser printer
- Leave a one inch margin left and right—the reader may want space to write comments
- Print some of the words in bold to emphasize, but do not use a variety of fonts.

Key Points

- Be sure to have all dates and names before starting your work
- Be short and to the point, stay on one page
- Use key words and action verbs
- Spell-check
- Review the resume with friends or family

7

My Cover Letter

The resume is a general description of yourself, whereas the cover letter covers the specific needs of the company you are addressing. It is similar to the Target letter (Chapter 12), but more focused on highlighting the ways in which you meet the company's requirements.

- Be sure you give your full name, address, email, and phone number
- Whenever possible, address letter to a person. For example, "Dear Mrs. Miller"
- The cover letter should be short—three of four paragraphs, less than a full page
- Use the keywords that the potential employer used in an ad
- End with "Sincerely,"

The content of the cover letter varies depending on why you are sending the letter.

By example: If it is follow-up to a networking meeting or to a personal solicitation, you start by thanking for the meeting and mentioning what seemed to be important.

Do not use empty statements such as "Please do not hesitate to call me if you have any questions." If they are interested in you they will call. If they are not interested, they will not have any questions.

The following sample cover letter would tie in with the resume A.

Sample Document 4

Cover Letter

Peter Smith
109 Maine Street,
St. Augustine, FL 32080
Phone (904) 940 1234
email psmith 222@yahoo.com

The Beach Hotel
Att. Ms. Betty Miller
PO Box 511
Kennebunk, ME 04043

Dear Ms. Miller,

Following up on our telephone conversation about the position of Head of Accounting, you find enclosed my resume and a letter of recommendation.

During the five years with the Wonderful Hotel, I created many helpful contacts with the most important vendors of food and hotel supplies in the region—I know most vendor's managers by name.

My major accomplishments were:

- Optimizing the cost of credit cards with a new processor

- Getting favorable payment conditions from the main suppliers
- Streamlining the payroll system
- Introduction of a tight cash control system for the restaurant and the gift shop
- Reducing dead inventory in the gift shop

A part of my responsibility was the handling of all billing complaints by hotel guests after check out. I was *congratulated* by the hotel management on my handling of this difficult job.

I am sure I could make a valuable contribution to the running of your hotel, and am looking forward to meeting you to explain why I want to change.

Sincerely yours,

Enclosures: Resume
Letter of recommendation.

8

The Five Ways to Get a Job

In the present economic condition, the total number of jobs available is shrinking. But there are still many openings, because employees retire, get sick or die, leave for another position, or get fired. There are also some companies that are still growing and hiring, for example in the health care industry and in government.

Over a million people are hired every month in the US—make sure you are one of them. When the economy gets back to normal again, that figure may be three million!

There are many people looking for open jobs. Employers get swamped with job offers.

You will most probably have to make a great number of applications to get an interview.

Success rate of various approaches

Here is our best estimate of how many activities it takes *to get a job interview.*

Networking meetings	10
The most successful way!	
Target letters	20
The intelligent way	
Personal solicitation	20
Use your personal touch	
Newspaper ads	50
Everybody's way	
Internet applications	100
The easy way, but little results	

When you have a first interview, you will normally need at least a second one before you are hired. You have one chance in three to get a second interview, and one chance in three to get hired after the second interview.

How long does it take?

Let us make some calculations. The figures we provide are averages, but you may be very clever or lucky and get a job much quicker. But do not count on it. Our figures are based on hundreds of cases.

If you strive to get two job offers, you most likely need six second interviews, or eighteen first interviews.

What does it take to get 18 first interviews? Look at the ratios given above, and how much job search activity is required to get these interviews.

With *networking* it takes 18 x 10 = 180 Networking meetings

With *Targetletters* or personal solicitation it takes 18 x 20 = 360 Target letters or personal contacts

With *Newspaper ads* it takes 18 x 50 = 900 applications

With *Internet applications* it takes 18 x 100 = 1800 applications

With a reasonable mix of the five approaches, it may take you 300 to 500 actions to reach your goal of 18 first interviews. If you make five contacts a day, that takes 60 to 100 days. If you work on it five days a week that means it will take you 12 to 20 weeks as a full time job. You may have quicker results, but it also may take you longer, depending what you are looking for, and how well you fit in.

This may look overwhelming. But please do not get discouraged. Everybody looking for a job has to live with this—you are not alone.

Plan to look for work for about twenty weeks or longer. *Do not give up!* Ask yourself how you are going to get through this difficult time, both psychologically and financially.

Here are some ways to get through it:

How to survive

Psychologically

If you feel discouraged after having made your work plan, you need support! Support can come from family and friends. Keep in touch with them, talk to them, and listen to them! Join a local group of job-seekers.

Financially

- Unemployment Insurance. If you have any questions or problems, you will find answers on the internet at "unemployment insurance benefits" for your state (example: Google: NY unemployment insurance")
- Food stamps. The internet address to find out if you qualify is www.fns.usda.gov/fsp/applicant_recepients/10 steps.htm."
- Temporary Work. There are local temporary work providers that you find in the yellow pages and on the internet. Temporary work is a good way to make new contacts, to determine if you like a company, and if they like you. Normally, you will not be hired directly after a temporary job, but you may apply later.

- Fill-in job. Take any part time job in any capacity. You may have to do things you do not like, or for which you are overqualified. But again: If you like the company and they like you, there may be an interesting opening. Do not take a full time fill-in job! You already have one: Looking for a job is a full time job!
- Volunteer Work does not bring you immediate income, but it puts your foot in the door if ever there is an opening for a paying position, and it also creates networking possibilities.

If you are over Fifty

Today, pension funds and health care coverage may or may not be part of your hiring package. Together with inflation, this means that you may have to work longer than your planned retirement age.

Begin now and get started!!

9

Getting the Job—
Networking Face to Face

Networking is the most important part of your job search. Over half of the successful job searchers find their new job through networking. Fortunately, you already are a networker.

Networking simply means asking people to share some information they possess.

You have done this all your life: You might have asked your sister about a babysitter, your neighbor about a boat, or a friend about a movie. Most of us already have lots of face-to-face networking experience.

Even so, you may find it difficult to start, so we recommend that you begin with easy contacts, such as relatives and friends. Soon you will grow in networking skill and confidence. But, let us warn you, it is time consuming.

Arranging Your Networking Interview

Most likely *none of your acquaintances will have a job for you*, but some may know about a job possibility, or know someone who has a useful connection.

An important consideration: If you ask someone to help you to find a job, the contact may honestly tell you "*I don't believe that I can help you*". But, because no one likes to refuse to help, they are likely to feel embarrassed by saying that they can't. To avoid this awkward situation, try this approach:

"Carol, you probably know that I am job hunting. I have a plan about how to do this, and have also prepared a resume. I'd like to get your opinion about it. Also, I believe you have some knowledge of the xyz industry, and might have some ideas as to how I can get more involved with them. Can I have about twenty minutes of your time? When would that be convenient for you?"

With this approach, you have asked your friend/relative for his or her *opinion*. Most of them will be flattered that you value their opinion, and will be happy to help.

When you prepare to meet someone for a networking interview, keep in mind three things:

1. You want the person to know that you are looking for a job, and the kind of a job you in which you are interested.

2. You want their opinion about your resume and on how to go about your job search
3. You want names of people that they know who could be of help to you. This is most important—it's how you add to your networking list. From each contact, *try to get at least one name and phone number.*

Before you make these calls, it's important that you have your resume completed and an outline of a job search plan. The next pages will help you to do this.

At Your Networking Interview

When greeting your contacts, tell them briefly the kind of a job you are looking for and show them your resume. Then, just listen and take notes. Taking notes shows that you value what your contact says.

Here are some questions you may want to ask:

- *"Here is my resume. Do you have any suggestions how I could make it better?"* You will probably get a lot of suggestions; many of them are likely to be useless. But do listen, you never know. If you work through this book, you will know more about resume writing than most people!

- *"I am looking into the XYZ industry. Do you know any specific company I should contact? Do you know anyone there?"*
- *Do you think I should extend my search to other industries? Which ones? Any specific company?"*
- *"Do you know anyone I should see?"* If they provide you with any names, ask: *"Can I mention that you gave me their name?"*
- *"How did you find your present job?"*

Before you leave, be certain to thank them for their time and to leave your business card (or at least your email or telephone number), asking them to contact you should they think of anyone else you could call.

Developing Networking Contacts

Anyone you know is a potential candidate for a networking interview. It is almost impossible to tell beforehand who will be helpful to you in your job search and who will not. The more calls you make, the greater the chance for a meaningful contact.

Here are some sources for names. Go through:

- Your address book and your email list
- Your Christmas card list

- The membership list of your clubs and associations
- The alumni list of your school and university
- Local newspapers and TV listings for Networking
- Parties and support groups organized by the Unemployment Office, churches, or the Chamber of Commerce

A checklist of other contact possibilities:

Family

Friends

Neighbors

Church Members

Lawyer

Clergy

Fraternity Members

Former bosses

Former Colleagues

Former customers

Former vendors or suppliers

Local support groups

"Pink slip" parties

If you are over Fifty

Networking is likely to be the most productive of all your job search efforts. Your age and life experiences have exposed you to a wide range of contacts—far more than younger job seekers. The approach outlined above will work well for you; no alterations will be needed. Again, older job seekers will gain most by putting more time and effort into networking than the other job search activities.

Secondary Networking Contacts

As your networking proceeds, you will be accumulating names of persons recommended by your initial network contact. You will not know these people and, in almost all cases, you will be calling them. Here's an approach that has worked well for many:

> *"Mr. Jones, my name is Jane Smith. Our mutual friend Joe Miller recommended that I call you about*..................(this can be an industry or a specific company) *and Joe said that you were quite knowledgeable about this industry and that you may be able to help me. Would you be kind enough to give me about 20 minutes of your time? When would this be convenient for you?"*

One unspoken objective of your meeting is the name of at least one other person for you to contact.

A Caution

In meetings with secondary contacts the procedure is the same as with your initial contact, except that you do not say that you are looking for a job. If you are asked why you want the information, indicate that, *"I'm in the midst of making a career change and I am looking at the company/ industry as a possibility for future employment."*

Keeping Track

Once you start networking, it will become immediately apparent that you will need some system for keeping track of names, email addresses, web sites, telephone numbers, and other relevant information.

There are several ways to do this:

- File cards
- Notebook list—hand written or on computer spread sheet
- A combination of the two.

File Cards: Many job-searchers like the versatility of cards—they can be sorted in convenient arrays such as geographic area, last name, industry, etc. Also, you do not need computer access to make use of them. A handy format for such cards is shown as Worksheet 7. These cards can be reproduced on most home printers.

Skillbuilder 7

Networking Contacts

File Cards

_____   _____   _____

Last Name   First Name   Title

Contact Date: ___/___/_____

_____ _____ _____

Telephone # Location: City State

Interesting Information: _____

_____

_____

_____

_____

_____

Source of Contact_____

Follow-up Date _____

Notebook Lists

Notebook lists are easy to use, but rarely have space for all the items listed in Skillbuilder 7. However, if you prefer a list, Worksheet 8 provides a ready to use format. You may find it more convenient or efficient to maintain your data on a computer spreadsheet.

Skillbuilder 8

Networking Contacts—Notebook Lists

Last Name   First Name
Ph #   mail address   *Date*

1. _____
   _____ / /

   Remarks:_____
   _____ / /

2. _____
   _____ / /

   Remarks:_____
   _____ / /

3. _____
   _____ / /

   Remarks:_____
   _____ / /

4. _____
   _____ / /

   Remarks:_____
   _____ / /

5. _____
   _____ / /

   Remarks:_____

```
                                                          /  /
 6.  _____
     _____  /  /

     Remarks:_____
                                                          /  /
 7.  _____
     _____  /  /

     Remarks:_____
                                                          /  /
 8.  _____
     _____  /  /

     Remarks:_____
                                                          /  /
 9.  _____
     _____  /  /

     Remarks:_____
                                                          /  /
10.  _____
     _____  /  /

     Remarks:_____
     _____  /  /
```

Key Points

- Networking is a key step in finding job—this is especially true for older, experienced persons.
- The two basic contact sources are:

    a. persons you know and any referrals they may give you

    b. contacts gathered from internet sources (discussed in the next chapter)

- An important strategy in obtaining networking interviews is to ask for information and help; not asking for direct assistance in finding a job.
- It is vital to keep up-to-date records about your contacts so that can organize and prioritize your calls/interviews and be efficient in taking appropriate follow-up steps.

10

Getting the Job—
Networking with the Internet

A great number of social networking websites are available. All together, over 30 million people are in at least one of them. These networks help you to make contacts with other jobseekers and to learn from them. But you can also find job opportunities that you had not considered before.

When you apply for a position, you are just one of many, maybe many hundred. But if you find somebody through networking who has a link to a target company and will recommend you, that lifts you above the crowd. Any hiring manager would rather hire somebody who has been recommended than somebody who just walked in. This reduces the danger of making a hiring mistake which can be costly (and also not good for the reputation of the hiring manager).

Very popular networking websites are LinkedIn, Facebook, and Myspace. They let you enter your profile. LinkedIn accepts only business related data, such as work experience and is therefore the most professional and most useful for job searching.

Keep in mind that all the information you put in one of the networks is public information. Anybody can access it—your family and your friends, your colleagues, employers and former employers, credit card companies, sales organizations—anybody. Juliette Powell, a career consultant, says it is like talking in a room with 33 million people in it. So think carefully what you are going to say.

LinkedIn asks you to give some personal professional information, and then offers you options about what you want to find. You would choose "finding a job", and maybe "Staying in contact with my colleagues and keeping informed of career moves". The next choice is what you should be contacted about. You certainly want "career opportunities", and perhaps some of the other options given.

Face book may be helpful, but is mainly for social contacts. You can put in your photo and a lot of personal information. It is useful to find people with whom you have lost contact, but now want to renew the relationship. They may be teachers or school acquaintances, former colleagues, former supervisors, or even long-time-no-see friends. This can be a valuable tool to extend your networking contacts.

Myspace is very similar to facebook.

Jobfox is a site that lets you network with potential employers.

We recommend putting yourself at least in LinkedIn.

Suggestions for Internet Networking

1. Consider getting an online account (email address) solely for networking use—especially if you use Facebook or Myspace. Otherwise, your regular email address could be inundated with unwanted messages and spam. You can easily set up a free new address on hotmail.com or yahoo.com.

2. When you encounter a blog or profile of someone online that has interests similar to yours, take the initiative and write to them. You will gain respect and a likely response if you first compliment them on what they've written. For example: "*I see that you've had a very interesting career in human resources—it's a little bit like mine.*".... This is much better than saying, "*Here's my resume. Can you help me?*"

3. Join an online discussion group (such as is offered on Linkedin). But, keep your contacts with members of the group on a one-on-one basis. Sending your newsletter or resume to the entire group will result in negative reactions.

4. Express appreciation to anyone who reaches out to you. A simple *"Thank you"* or *"I really appreciate your help"* keeps them as your friend and may result in additional support.

11

Getting the Job—Personal Solicitation

Means of Communication

Nothing beats personal contact. There are three options:

- *Personal visits:* The best way to communicate is eye to eye, because you can see the reaction of your discussion partners, you can see if they follow you, believe you and agree, or if they have some doubts or disagreement. Visual contact allows you to modify your approach.

- *Telephone conversation* is the second best communication. In a telephone conversation you cannot see your partner, but you can still check reactions by asking questions such as: *"Do you agree with me? What do you think about this?"*

- *Written communication* (Target letter) is the weakest, because what you write is final. There is no way to modify or correct it. This is why all written communication must be very carefully worded. Obviously, this holds true for resumes, letters, emails, and other internet communications.

Excellent sources for personal contacts are the Yellow Pages. Once you have determined your geographical area and the industry you are looking for, search for the companies to personally contact. Then you either go there or you make a phone call.

Personal Visits

For smaller companies, *it is best to go there in person* and find out if they are hiring. Even if they are not at this very moment, you can leave your card and your resume. You may be looking for weeks, and during that time, their situation may change. So be sure you leave a positive image. And write a follow up letter the same day. This letter may say:

Dear Ms. Doe,

Thank you for talking with me today. I liked the vitality of your company and what you told me about it. I believe I could make a significant contribution to your team.

I would appreciate you contacting me if you have any need in the future.

Sincerely yours,

Enclosure: My resume

Contacts by phone

The second best networking effort is to make a personal contact by phone. Depending on the size of the company and the kind of a position you are looking for, you may want to talk to the owner of the company, the head of the department that could use you, or the Human Resources manager. Be short.

"My name is Joe Burton. I am looking for a position as master electrician, but I am also a good general maintenance man. Are you hiring at the present time?"

If the answer is negative, say

"I am very interested in working for your company. Can I send you my resume, in case you would have an opening in the future?"

Be sure to write a follow up letter the same day.

Your letter could say:

Dear Mr. Smith,

Thank you for talking to me on the phone. As an experienced master electrician, I could certainly be of value to you. Please keep my resume on file and contact me when you have an opening.

Sincerely yours,

Enclosure: my resume

12

Getting the Job— Target Letters

Target letters to Department Managers

Once you have decided in what city or area you want a job, you have to develop a list of companies you would like to work with. The Yellow Pages are the best source for this, but there are also other sources. You can check:

- Your library for address books about specific industries.
- The Chamber of Commerce.
- The Internet. Enter in the Yellow Pages, the industry or kind of business, and the desired city.

Once you have your list of companies, you can approach them with Target Letters.

The best use of Target Letters is not to approach the human resources department, but the head of the department you are interested it. Here is why:

When department heads require additional manpower, they normally know for some time about their need before they take action. When they decide to do something about it, they need a budget and an approval from their superior. Once they have this, they ask Human Resources to look for someone. Human Resources will have to create a job description or update an existing one, and decide how they are going to look for the future employee. From the time the managers know that they need somebody, to the moment the Human Resources actively looks for someone, may take weeks; in large organizations sometimes months.

If you find a manager who has a need for a new employee, you are in an excellent position, because there is no competition, and you will be able to talk directly to your potential boss.

How do you find the manager of the department where you want to work? The best way is to get a name through networking.

If you were not successful with this, call the company and say to the telephone operator/receptionist:

> *"I have to write a letter to the head of your maintenance department. Could you please give me his name? Could you please spell it for me?"*

Now you have what you need, and can write your letter. The letter should be short, and just give enough information to invite some questions. Do not attach your resume, or the letter my go to the Human Resources Department, and that is not what you want.

Sample Document 5

Target Letter

John Doe
Mayflower Street 15
Downshill, NY 12092
Phone (102) 201 1234
Email joedoe3212@yahoo.com

November 5, XXXX

The Uphill Company
Attention of Mr. Joe Doe
PO Box 512
Townsville, FL 45045

Dear Mr. Doe,

I have ten years experience as a maintenance technician. I have an electrician's license, and have done mechanical maintenance of printing and copying equipment.

Due to the downsizing of my present employer, I am looking for a position.

Some of my recent accomplishments include:

- Installation of two big HP electronic control systems in very short time

- Finishing two classes in advanced electronics at the Suny Institute
- Was honored as the most valuable employee in 2006 by my employer

I would appreciate discussing with you the contributions I could make to your operation, and will give you a call next week to arrange a meeting.

Sincerely yours,

Five to seven days after you send your Target letter, give the recipient a call and try to arrange an interview. Hopefully, you may be asked to submit a resume—a good sign. You should call again five to seven days after you sent the resume.

Target Letters to Employment Agencies and Headhunters

These letters are similar to the Target Letter, but you tell them *where you want to work and include your resume*.

You find addresses of employment agencies in newspapers and in the yellow pages.

Head Hunters mainly handle positions that pay over $150,000. You find them in the yellow pages under "Executive Search Firms" or in the "Directory of Executive Recruiters" (you are likely to find it in your local library).

13

Getting the Job—Newspaper Ads

Answering a newspaper or magazine ad needs a cover letter and your resume. The cover letter is important. Many applicants just send a resume, but a resume only provides general information.

Every ad will be answered by many applicants. You have to find a way to distinguish yourself, so your application gets attention.

In your cover letter you should respond to the specifics of the job. Here is a typical ad:

Sales Account Executive

We are looking for a *highly motivated* Account Executive to solicit new advertising business from newspaper advertisers.

> Excellent *customer service, sales, and conflict-resolution* skills required. Must be able to *work independently*, and have *computer proficiency*. Must have *reliable transportation* and a *valid driver's license*.
>
> Please send your resume to…

The person who wrote this ad put some effort into wording it. Highlight or underline, in the ad, the words they use to tell you what they want. This is what we did in the ad above. Then, use these words in your letter. Your answer to the above ad could read like this:

Sample Document 6

Application to a Newspaper Ad

Peter Smith
109 Maine Street
St. Augustine, FL 32080
Phone (904) 940 1234
email psmith 222@yahoo.com

The Beach Hotel
Att. Ms. Betty Miller
PO Box 511
Kennebunk, ME 04043

Re: Your ad "Sales Account Executive" in the…Newspaper

I have eight years of successful experience in customer service as sales executive for the Manitoba Advertising company and think I could make a significant contribution to your company's sales.

I have worked independently, mainly from my home, and was in steady contact through my computer with the head office. I am proficient in Word, Excel, and Power Point. I drive my own car, and have a Florida Drivers License.

In 2005 and 2007 I was the best salesman at Manitoba and I am strongly motivated to perform the same way in your company. I am leaving Manitoba because a family situation requires me to locate to your area.

The enclosed resume gives you more details about my background.

Looking forward to meeting you,

Sincerely yours,

If you know the company, *call about ten days after* you send the letter and ask for an interview.

14

Getting the Job— Internet Applications

The Internet is the most popular job search instrument with a great number of possibilities.

You enter your target job, and the web site will show you what jobs are available. Depending what you are looking for you may find only a few or hundreds of jobs.

You apply for the jobs you are interested in by entering your profile and your resume.

Easy—is it not?

But: Tens of thousands of job searchers are using this tool, and your chance of being selected, your chance of success, is very small.

You should certainly use this tool, but remember that all the other tools have a much better success rate.

There are more than thousand job search websites. We found the following most reliable:

- *www.Monster.com* is very complete and gives you the chance to enter your profile and your resume once, and will use it for all your applications.
- *www.Indeed.com* You cannot put in a resume, but this is a search engine that gives you access to a great number of job possibilities
- *www.CareerBuilder.com* lets you put in a resume. The program gives you a good list of job search communities.
- *www.USAjobs.gov* and go to "Job Search." It shows you over 40,000 government job opportunities. You can enter up to five different resumes, depending on the job you are applying for.

There are two other ways to take advantage of the internet:

- Go to *www.Google.com* and put in what you are looking for, either geographically or by industry, such as "Miami FL jobs", "Hotel jobs" or "Accounting jobs", or a specific company name.
- If you know companies you would like to work for, go to their web site. Many companies have a heading such as: "jobs", "careers," or "employment", in which they list all the open jobs.

Most internet programs ask you for a resume. Some ask you to fill in a form, others ask you to send a resume that you already have in your computer.

Some programs give you the possibility of adding a cover letter. Take advantage of this. It is a great way to show how you can exactly fill what the company is looking for. Use the same technique when answering newspaper ads (see chapter 13).

If you know the address of the company you are applying to, you can considerably increase your chance of being considered by sending your cover letter and your resume via snail mail (even though you already provided it online). It presents much better than the one you sent over the internet, and it may be exposed to more people in the organization. It is definitely worthwhile to do this.

If you are over Fifty

One worthwhile internet program to look up is www. retirementjobs.com. It has many programs and ideas. We recommend you become a premium member, and follow their weekly internet/telephone conferences.

They work together with AARP, which you can find at www.aarp.org/money/personal/real_relief_aarp.

15

My Work Plan

Finding a job is a full time job! We told you this at the beginning, but here is the proof. Below is a typical weekly work plan.

Phone calls for:

Networking interviews	10
To follow up on letters and emails	10
For personal solicitations	5
To employment agencies and search companies	2
Total phone calls	*27*

Letters and emails

Target letters	10
Follow up on interviews and networking	9
Internet applications	10

Newspaper ads 5
Total Letters and emails — *34*

Meetings

Networking — 5
Personal solicitations — 3
Interviews — 2

Total Meetings — *10*

Total Activities per week — *71*

Skillbuilder 9

My Workplan

Week	1	2	3	4	5	6	7	8
Phone calls								
For Networking								
Follow up								
Personal Solicitation								
Empl Agencies								
Letters, emails								
Target letters								
Follow ups								
Internet applications								
Newspaper ads								
Personal Solicitation								
Meetings								
Networking								
Personal Solicitation								
Interviews								
Total activities								

Record keeping

With all these activities, you will have many, many contacts and will see quite a few people. You will not be able to remember all the names and details of your discussions. It is important—from the very beginning—that you take notes and keep them organized. You can do this in a notebook, on your computer, or on file cards.

For most people, large 5x8" file cards are the most practical because you can take them with you and fill them in right after a meeting. You can arrange them in any sequence you want: geographically, alphabetically, or by date of next action necessary.

We suggest you have two kinds of cards, one for Networking Contacts, and one for Company Contacts.

Skillbuilder 10

Networking Contact Card

Networking Contacts, front of card

Name _____

Home address_____

_____

Home Phone_____

Cellphone_____

Email address_____

Business address_____

Business phone_____

Business Fax_____

Remarks_____

_____

Networking Contacts, back of card

Under Action, use L for letter, E for Email, F for fax, P for phone, V for visit

Date	Action	Summar	Next Step

Skillbuilder 11

Company Contact Card

Company Contacts, front of card

Company Name_____

Address_____

Phone_____

Fax_____

Email_____

Important people: Names and Titles_____

_____

Annual Sales $_____

Trends_____

_____

Documents consulted _____

Company Contacts, back of card

Under Action, use L for letter, E for Email, F for fax, P for phone, V for visit

Date   Action   Contact Person   Next Action/Date

_____

_____

_____

_____

_____

_____

_____

_____

16

My Job Interview

Congratulations! You have an interview coming up.

All the hard work you did up to now could not get you a job, but it gave you the opportunity for an interview—the key step to getting the job.

What an opportunity! Think of it: Out of as few as thirty or as many as several hundred candidates, you were selected (perhaps with a few others) to be interviewed.

Now you need to have a better interview than the few others who will be interviewed. This chapter will prepare you to show your potential employer that you are the best candidate.

The interview not only gives your potential interviewer a chance to evaluate you, but it also represents an opportunity for you to evaluate your eventual employer and to decide if you want the job being considered.

Here are some questions you may want to ask (if the answers were not already provided):

- Who will I report to?
- What kind of training will I receive?
- Is there a trial period?
- Work hours
- Salary, commission
- Health insurance and perks
- Vacation
- Dress code

Research the company. The more you know about the company when you go to see them, the better impression you will make. Your interviewers will be impressed to see that you did your homework and researched their organization.

Sources for information about a company are

- The internet, especially for bigger companies
- Local newspapers
- Yellow pages
- Your network

A helpful perspective:

This chapter will make the most sense to you when you appreciate a truism—most interviewers don't know how to evaluate you! Yes, you read that right. Think of it this way. If your education and/or work experience weren't adequate, you wouldn't have been invited for the interview. Now that you're here for the interview, your interviewer has the problem of translating your background into *how* you will perform on the job. This poses a significant problem for most interviewers. So, we will help them with this task; we will show you how to assist the interviewer in "discovering" your strengths and how you go about working.

Another perspective:

Clearly, your interview is the time to sell yourself. To do that most effectively, you need to have a prepared list of attributes that you can easily communicate. To be certain that your strengths are in areas important to the interviewer, we are providing, below, a description of four key factors that account for success in most jobs. We will help you learn how to convey strengths in each of these factors.

Factors That Account for Success at Work

Know-how:

Skill Builder 12 can help you develop your list.

Includes all you've learned from your educational background, work experiences, and life experiences. For example,

> *"My ten years experience with headquarters' buyers should enable me to develop a really effective key account campaign."*

> *"My broad experience in IT should let me quickly adapt to your systems."*

Intellect:

Refers to your intellectual capabilities in two dimensions—natural aptitudes (e.g., quantitative, verbal, mechanical, artistic) and how you usually go about thinking. For example, you might be someone who thinks quickly on your feet, or thinks in a logical, systematic manner, or thinks in a creative, intuitive way, etc.). Here are two examples:

"Math always came easily to me.""

"I seem to have good conceptual ability. I usually look at problems from a broad perspective."

Personality:

This factor has to do with how you interact with others and how you typically behave. For example:

> *"I find that I have good ability to relate to people at all levels in a company. I'm interested in others and I think they sense that."*
>
> *"One time, in a performance appraisal, my boss said that one of my best qualities is dependability—that he could count on me…that if I said I would do something, it would get done."*

Motivation:

This factor has to do with your interests (activities you enjoy doing), your drive, and your energy level. Here are some examples:

[Interests] *"I've always been a hands-on person. I enjoy working with equipment and machinery."*

[Drive] *"I've always been a self-starter. I have a strong need to achieve--to accomplish things."*

[Energy] *"I have a high energy level—I can work long hours without tiring."*

At the end of this chapter Skillbuilder 12 can help you to develop your list

Here's Your Interview Strategy:

Eye contact:

Look your interviewers in the eyes when you meet and keep frequent eye contact during the interview. You don't want to stare, but looking away frequently might be interpreted by interviewers that you are not sure of yourself.

Convey Your Strengths:

In a nutshell, you're going to try to convey to the interviewer *at least* five positive attributes—items that make you effective at work.

From the four factors that account for job success (listed above), we will show you how to develop two positive attributes from the "Know-how" factor and one from each of the other three factors. During the interview, you want to be able to describe these attributes confidently and without any embarrassment.

How to Communicate Your Strengths

As you'll see, during the interview, there are two basic opportunities for helping your interviewer learn about your good qualities: (A) when you respond to direct questions and (B) when you are discussing your background.

A. In Response to Interviewer's Questions

Described below are some frequently asked questions that can provide a "springboard" from which you can mention your positive qualities.

1. *"What are some of your strengths?"* A question like this provides a wonderful opportunity to sell yourself.

Take advantage of it! You need to be careful, however, not to sound egotistical or conceited, so select only *three* items to share in response this question. You'll weave in a couple of others elsewhere during the interview. It is important to rehearse your answer to this question so that it doesn't come across as "canned." You want to convey the image of first thinking about the question and then slowly coming up with your answer.

Here's an example:

> *"I'm not sure what to say. But, as I look back over my accomplishments a few strengths do stand out. First, I think that I have good verbal skills—I find it easy to communicate in writing or in face-to-face situations. For example, giving presentations is something I can do quite well. I also seem to have a high energy level—I can work long hours and not get tired. One other strength I can think of is that my last boss said that he was impressed with my persistence--that I don't get easily discouraged. "Sticking to it" was important in that job because our division was facing some difficult obstacles. Are these the kind of things you're looking for?"*

2. *Why should we hire you?* Respond to this gem in much the same way as for question #1. However, here you try to tailor your response to whatever you

have learned about the organization's needs. For example, if the interviewer seems to be focusing on your past work experiences, it is important to include, as one of your strengths, a job-related attribute or special expertise.

For instance, *"I've had great success in credit and collections, and I'm confident that I can significantly reduce your accounts receivables."*

3. *Tell me about yourself.* This is one of the most difficult inquiries to respond to. For most interviewers *what* you say in your response is not as important as *how* you handle it. The most frequent tendency is to say too much. Applicants often give too much detail—they bore the interviewer, go off on tangents, or reveal information about them that is better left unsaid.

Despite the difficulty in managing your answer, the "tell me about yourself" statement provides another opportunity to present some strengths. However, *this is a response that must be rehearsed.* You want to come across as organized and concise. Here's how to do it:

You use a strategy that we call three steps and a bridge. They are:

a. Your early background (e.g., where you were brought up)

b. Your education

c. Your work experience

d. A bridging statement such as, "...and that background brings me here today for this job."

The idea is to touch briefly on each of the first three areas and, for each, point out a significant achievement and, if possible, mention a positive strength that accounted for the success. You end up with the bridging phrase. Here's an example:

[Background] "I was brought up in family of five boys. We were a close family, but competitiveness was something you learned early on if you wanted things to go your way.

[Education] In high school I was quite good at math and liked the science courses

After high school, I went to Case-Western Reserve University and got a BS in mechanical engineering. I did well academically, making the Dean's list seven out of my eight semesters. While there, I discovered that I wasn't afraid to speak up at class meetings and that led to my being elected VP of our junior class and President of the senior class.

[Work Experience] After graduating, I took a job at Allied Chemical, starting in their management training program. After two years, I found myself involved in a production

control problem for which I was able to develop a solution—a computerized program. Soon after, I was moved up to a supervisory position. One year later, I was contacted by a headhunter who told me of a unique opportunity at Perkin-Elmer Corporation—they wanted someone with high-tech production experience and computer expertise. The job attracted me because it gave me a chance to advance in management and also to work on the development of new equipment.

I have been at Perkin-Elmer now for three years as assistant manager of technical development…

[Bridge]…and it's this combination of engineering experience, IT know-how, and management skills that leads me to the position we are discussing here today."

In almost every instance, you will find that an answer of this sort, which takes only two minutes, makes a positive impression

Since the "tell me about yourself" question is frequently asked, and because it is so crucial, it is imperative that you *develop* your answer before taking any interviews. You will need to practice saying it aloud. To help you in developing your response, see Skillbuilder 13 at the end of this chapter.

4. *What Are Your Major Weaknesses or Limitations?* It's hard to imagine that this question can be a vehicle for conveying your attributes, but it's possible.

   However, before we discuss how to do that, let's first recognize that this question is often phrased in more subtle ways, usually in an effort to make the question appear less threatening. You might, for example, hear the question stated this way:

   "What are some areas in which you can improve?"
   "How have you grown over the years?"
   "Where do you see yourself needing to grow in the near future?"

   OK, let's get back to answering this question. Two basic techniques work:

   1. Mention a weakness that comes about because you over-use one of your strengths.
   2. Mention weaknesses that are easily remedied.

   For all of us, our weaknesses almost always stem from relying too heavily on our strengths. For example, if your nature is such that you are fast-paced and action-oriented, very likely some of your strengths are decisiveness, ability to multi-task, and ability to accomplish much in a short period of time. However, when you over-rely on your fast-paced behavior, you are apt to be seen as impatient, not well-organized, or one who does not pay enough attention to details. What behavior do you get complimented for? What happens if it is over-used?

When you prepare to answer the "shortcomings" question, select one of your strengths and then mention how, *because of the attribute,* a particular shortcoming is evident. For example:

> *"I tend to look at issues from a 'big picture' point of view and sometimes I am accused of not paying enough attention to details."*
>
> *"I'm a Type A, action-oriented person and I'm inclined to show my impatience with those who move more slowly than me. But, I'm working on this."*

A second suggestion is to mention something that is easily remedied. For instance:

> *"I want to broaden my managerial skills. I've been reading some of Peter Drucker's books, and I plan to start working on my MBA this fall by taking evening courses."*
>
> *"I need to improve my presentation skills. I am planning to sign up for the next Toastmaster's course."*

Skillbuilder 14 provides guidance in preparing yourself for this question.

B. During Discussion of Your Background

As your interviewer opens various topics such as work history and educational background, opportunities abound for revealing your strengths.

You accomplish this by converting five or six strengths (from the Job Success Factors described earlier in this chapter) into one-line descriptions of each strength. These one-liners are usually "hooked" onto an achievement that is being discussed. For instance:

> *"Yes, I was elected president of the fraternity.* [one-liner] *I seem to be able to relate well to all kinds of people."*
>
> *"What helped me most on that job was developing a strong staff*—[one-liner] *I've found that I have a knack for teaching."*

We realize that many people feel uncomfortable talking about their good qualities. But how else can you be sure that the interviewer will understand your strengths? Most interviewers focus on finding what is not good about you; here's the chance to offer the counterbalance.

Skillbuilder 13 provides help in developing skill in the use of one-liners.

If you are over Fifty

Quite often, your interviewers will be significantly younger than you. As they probe and challenge, they could come across as not being respectful of your age and/or your achievements. Most seniors will need to psychologically prepare themselves for this reality and guard against appearing resentful or "superior."

An issue of concern for many interviewers (but rarely spoken), is the problem of a generation gap—your ability to fit in with a much younger work group. You can counter this concern by subtly weaving into the interview how you are in touch with current lifestyles via your high school/college age children, working with local community, church, or civic groups that are largely comprised of younger people, etc.

On a positive note, you can use your broad work experience as a vehicle for demonstrating your adaptability and flexibility (an issue that might be of concern to some younger interviewers). Think about situations in which you successfully adapted to a quickly changing job demand or environment. For example, discuss how you quickly adjusted when a new boss came on the scene with a different management style and radically changed the department's organization.

Additional Guidelines for Standing Out Among the Competition

1. *Use the Skillbuilders* in this chapter to prepare yourself to effectively convey your strengths, particularly the "one-liner" statements.

2. *Watch your body language.* Try to maintain good posture without appearing stiff. Sit in a comfortable position and curtail any nervous habits (such as running your fingers through your hair or touching jewelry or blouse buttons with your fingers). Communicate your interest and attentiveness through frequent eye contact.

3. *Let your natural personality come through.* Do not try to be somebody you are not. It is extremely difficult to play a role, and if you do, your interviewer will likely pick up on it. You just won't "ring true."

4. *Consistently project positiveness and enthusiasm.* There may be occasional exceptions to this principle, but it almost always holds true. When the interviewer discusses the company, the job, the challenges, or problems that lie ahead, *overt enthusiasm* is vital. If you attitude isn't positive about these topics during an employment interview, the interviewer will assume that you certainly won't be positive about them at work.

Some applicants who are naturally reticent and controlled may experience difficulty in outwardly expressing enthusiasm. Internally they may feel quite positive, but you would never know it from observing them. If you are one of these persons, then it is especially important to use feeling words to help outwardly express your inner enthusiasm. For example:

> *"I am really excited about the challenges this job offers."*
> *"I feel very enthusiastic about all that I've seen thus far."*
> *"I can't wait to get started on a project like that."*

Remember, too, that people who appear stiff and controlled can project a more positive image by smiling more often and by emphasizing their thoughts through more frequent use of hand gestures.

5. *Don't be afraid to pause.* Whenever you are confronted with a thought-provoking question, there is no need to come up with an instant response. Take time to think about what you want to say. Pauses of this sort convey recognition of the importance of the interviewer's question; you appear confident and mature. Your pause also minimizes the risk of your answers coming across as "canned".

6. *Be open and honest* about the negative aspects of your career history. Instead of denying the obvious, acknowledge the weakness and turn it into an asset. The principle is to show how the limitation has led you to make a positive change or to acquire compensating strengths. Here are a few examples:

   > *"Yes, I have had a number of job changes, but they have been the very steps that helped me to learn what is right for me and what I can best do. The job here is exactly what I want, and I'm now ready to settle down and grow with a company such as yours."*
   >
   > Or
   >
   > *"It is true that I haven't had extensive experience in that area, but I am eager to learn. There might be an advantage in my being trained in your particular ways. At least, I won't have to unlearn practices that don't fit well here."*
   >
   > Or
   >
   > *"I do agree that sometimes I react too quickly, but I'm aware of that tendency and I'm working on it. The upside is that I can handle several projects at one time and not get rattled."*

7. After every interview, *review how it went*. As soon as you leave an interview, you're likely to begin mentally rehashing what occurred—consciously or unconsciously. It's hard to avoid second-guessing,

wondering, *"Should I have said more about this? Less about that?"* If you wanted the job, the self-questioning is almost inevitable. But, that's OK. Just as sport teams review previous game films, so you can use your review as an opportunity to improve your interviewing skills. Here's how to make your rehash productive:

a. *Review what went well and what didn't go so well.*

Understanding these two aspects of your interview is key to improving chances for success during the next one. We highly recommend that you record your analysis, using Skillbuilder 15. Writing your view of the interview will produce far better results than simply mulling them over in your mind.

Here are a few questions to consider as you rehash the interview:

- What information about myself (talents, experiences, traits) did the interviewer react favorably to?
- What did I say about myself that did not seem to make a favorable impression?
- If I could do the interview over, what, if anything, would I do differently?

- What appealed to me about the job? The organization?
- What did I hear about the job/organization that was not appealing?
- What is the best next step for me to take now with regard to this job opportunity?

b. *Record names.*

This is particularly important if several individuals interviewed you. If you are invited back for another interview, it will be invaluable to have the following information about each interviewer:

- Name and how they prefer to be called ("Mrs. Jones" or "Sally")
- Role in the organization
- Priorities—what was important to this person
- Reactions to you—what interviewer seemed to like/dislike

c. *Complete next steps.*

If you have scheduled interviews with more than one company, it is easy to slip up on follow-through items. For example, perhaps during the interview you were asked to name some references, and you want to prepare these people for the forthcoming reference call. Or, you may have made a commitment to the interviewer to send supplementary materials or to call on a particular date.

Jotting these kinds of items on Skillbuilder 15 helps ensure that nothing gets overlooked.

d. *Be cautious* in answering the question, *"What are your salary expectations?"* Given today's tight job market, it is easy to feel desperate. You might be tempted to say you're willing to *"take anything"* or you're willing to *"take a big salary cut from your last job"*. Such statements, however, create problems. You could easily be seen as a weak negotiator or someone who will leave for better money once the job market improves.

Instead, simply convey the idea that you'd like to be treated fairly for your experience and training. Rod McGovern, CEO of Jobfox suggests that you say something like this: "*I know these are difficult economic times, so I'm really just looking to be treated fairly in relation to my peers. I'm confident that, over time, your company will value my skill and contributions and that they will be reflected in my compensation.*"

Key Points

- To stand out above your job competitors, you need to sell yourself.

- You help sell yourself when you maintain good eye contact with your interviewer, sit erect, and outwardly express interest and enthusiasm. You standout out over other applicants when you help the interviewer learn about your strengths by conveying "one-liners" each of which describes a positive attribute.

- The interview is also an opportunity to learn about the job and company.

- It's important to have at least one one-liner for each of four factors—know how, intellect, personality, and motivation.

- The two basic opportunities for you to weave in these one-liners are:

    a. In response to interviewer's questions such as: *"Why should we hire you?" "Tell me about yourself." "What are your major weaknesses?"*

    b. During discussion of your background

- Let your personality come through. Don't try to be someone you are not.

- Consistently project positiveness and enthusiasm
- After each interview, review what went well and what did not. Do this in writing
- Record names of individuals you meet during the interview day.
- Make use of Worksheets to gain skill in using the concepts presented in this chapter

Skillbuilder 12

Cataloging Your Strengths
Developing "One-Liners"

In the spaces below, list two or three strengths in each of the four key factors: intellect, know-how, personality, and motivation. Since you won't know which of these factors is most important to your interviewer, it's important to include at least one strength for each category. Try to write them so that each can be described in one short sentence. We call them "one-liners".

INTELLECT FACTOR. Your natural intellectual aptitudes (e.g., "words come easily to me." "I have a great aptitude for math.") and *how* you typically process your thoughts (e.g., "I can think quickly on my feet." "I tend to be analytical—I like to think in a logical, systematic way.")

1. [Natural Aptitudes] _____
   _____
   _____

2. [How I tend to think/solve problems] _____
   _____
   _____

KNOWLEDGE/EXPERIENCE FACTOR. What you know very well (e.g., "I can quickly estimate materials from blueprints.") And, exceptional experience (e.g., "I've had ten years of increasingly responsible sales management experience, my last position being Director of Sales.")

1. [Knowledge/Expertise]. _____
   _____
   _____

2. [Good work experience in…] _____
   _____
   _____

PERSONALITY FACTOR. Think about interpersonal skills (e.g., "I'm not afraid to step in and take charge.") Also, helpful behavior patterns (e.g., "I find that I can gain quick acceptance from employees at all levels.")

1. [Interpersonal skills] (makes me effective in relating to others) _____
   _____
   _____

2. [Typical, effective behavior patterns] _____
   _____
   _____

MOTIVATION FACTOR. Include your interests (e.g., "I like jobs that keep my physically active and on-the-go.") Your drive (e.g., "My goal is to be a district manager within two years.") Your energy level (e.g., "I can work long hours without tiring").

1. [Interests] _____
   _____
   _____

2. [Drive] _____
   _____
   _____

3. [Energy level] _____
   _____
   _____

You probably feel good after cataloging all those assets. Hopefully you awareness of them will boost your confidence in your next interview. Seek every opportunity to weave these strengths into your interview.

If you listed six or more attributes, now go back and circle the four or five that you believe will have the most positive impact. Make sure, though, that you have at least one for each factor. Then practice saying these attributes until they can be spoken easily and confidently, in a concise, one-liner format.

Skillbuilder 13

Shaping Answers to the Invitation: "Tell Me About Yourself"

Remember our strategy for your answer: three steps and a bridge.

STEP 1. Very briefly discuss your early background.
Where were you brought up? _____

_____

_____

_____

Any interesting and relevant facts about your parents/family or early achievements (sports, scouts, awards, etc). If nothing strikes you as significant, skip comments on this item.

_____

_____

_____

_____

STEP 2. Describe your education:
If you are a college grad or have an advanced degree, skip comments about high school unless you had some significant achievement (graduated cum laude, etc.). If you are not a college grad, select only those aspects of high school

that reveal outstanding strengths such as writing, math, or leadership skills:

High School: _____

_____

_____

College/graduate school: _____

_____

_____

STEP 3. Discuss your work experiences:

Mention only job title, company, and one or two significant achievements. Very briefly explain the reason for any changes in employer (if the reason is positive, e.g., "was recruited away by another firm"). If you have a long work history, you don't need to mention more than the job title for early, less important positions.

If you are going for your first full-time job, name any part-time positions that will help you mention a skill or experience that might be meaningful to your interviewer.

First job: _____

[Any significant achievements?] _____

_____

_____

_____

I left because: _____

Second job: _____

[Any significant achievements?] _____

I left because: _____

Third job: _____

[Any significant achievements?] _____

I left because: _____

Skillbuilder 14

Answering the "Weaknesses" Question

Developing a good answer to this question takes some practice. The exercise below will guide in successfully managing it.

SHORTCOMING #1: _____

_____

_____

How will I phrase it? (Remember to state the "upside" of the weakness first.

_____

_____

_____

Now, read it over. Does your statement—

a. Suggest that the limitation is simply an overplay of a strength?
b. Sound like something that can easily be corrected or changed?

You should be able to answer yes" to either a or b. If you cannot, then you need to revise your answer.

It is good practice to have a second shortcoming ready in case your interviewer presses you, write one more.

SHORTCOMING #2: _____

_____

_____

How will I phrase it?

_____

_____

_____

Does it fulfill either criterion a or b?

If you rehearse these answers (say them aloud to friend or spouse), you'll be ready for this question during your next interview.

Skillbuilder 15

Lessons From Your Interview

Now that your interview is over, writing about your observations can help you become more successful in your next one. This Worksheet provides an excellent way to debrief yourself after each interview.

My Interview

Interview Date ____/____/_____

Name of Company _____

Job Title _____

Names of Interviewers _____

Your Interviewer's Reactions

My interviewer seemed to be impressed by my talents/experience/traits/attitude] Be specific:

1. _____
2. _____
3. _____

Some things I said or did that did *not* seem to favorably impress my interviewer were:

1. _____
2. _____
3. _____

Your Impressions

What appealed to me about the job/organization [pay, opportunity to learn, advancement potential, etc.]?

1. _____
2. _____
3. _____

What aspects of the job/organization were least appealing?

1. _____
2. _____
3. _____

Considering my experiences during this interview, what have I learned that I can use during my next one?

_____
_____
_____

What can I do, specifically, to make my next interview even more effective?

1. _____
   _____
2. _____
   _____

You might find it profitable to share this review with a friend, an outplacement counselor or an executive recruiter. They may have additional constructive suggestions for improvement.

17

My start in the New Company

Congratulations! You have successfully looked for a job and found one. Let us make sure you can keep it! Here are some guidelines:

- *Listen, learn, and be modest.* Each company has procedures and rules you may not understand or may not like. But this company was successful before you came. You will have to adapt to the new company—the company will not adapt to you! If you have ideas how things could be done better, wait a month or two before suggesting them.

- *The most important person is your supervisor.* Be sure you understand what he or she wants you to do, and keep in close contact. After two weeks, ask how pleased they are with your performance.

- *Use the first 100 days.* Everybody understands that you have to learn and understand the new job. Ask questions and be sure you understand the answers. Do not be shy about asking. It is better to ask "dumb" questions than to make dumb mistakes. Make sure you know everything you should know, because after a month or two you are supposed to know.

- *Open your ears!* Besides the official channels of communication, there are others—word of mouth you can pick up at the coffee machine or the central photocopier. Do not participate in the gossip, but listen to it.

- *Know the people!* There is a chain of command, but often there are other people that are very important: secretaries, manager's assistances, relatives of the boss.

- *Look for promotion possibilities!*

Be Alert.

Keep in mind, that while you were hired with the best intentions, your job is not guaranteed. Changes in the economy, the failure of a major product, or other circumstances may force the company to let you go. So keep your eyes open for other job possibilities.

We wish you much success in your new job.

Jurg Oppliger and John Drake